LYNX

Joyce James

Grolier
an imprint of

www.scholastic.com/librarypublishing

Published 2008 by Grolier
An imprint of Scholastic Library Publishing
Old Sherman Turnpike, Danbury,
Connecticut 06816

For The Brown Reference Group plc
Project Editor: Jolyon Goddard
Copy-editors: Ann Baggaley, Tom Jackson
Picture Researcher: Clare Newman
Designers: Jeni Child, Lynne Ross,
    Sarah Williams
Managing Editor: Bridget Giles

Volume ISBN-13: 978-0-7172-6268-7
Volume ISBN-10: 0-7172-6268-5

**Library of Congress
Cataloging-in-Publication Data**

Nature's children. Set 3.
    p. cm.
    Includes bibliographical references and
index.
    ISBN 13: 978-0-7172-8082-7
    ISBN 10: 0-7172-8082-9
    1. Animals--Encyclopedias, Juvenile. I.
    Grolier Educational (Firm)
    QL49.N384 2008
    590.3--dc22
                    2007031568

Printed and bound in China

PICTURE CREDITS

Front Cover: **Nature PL**: Jose B. Ruis.

Back Cover: **Alamy**: Blinkwinkel, Stockfolio;
Nature PL: Niall Benvie; **Shutterstock**:
Webtrias.

Alamy: Claudia Adams 41; **Corbis**: W. Perry
Conway 21, Robert Pickett 26–27; **Nature
PL**: John Cancalosi 14, Mary McDonald
46, Lynn M. Stone 22, Tom Vezo 38,
Dave Watts 17; **NHPA**: Andy Rouse 6;
Photolibrary.com: Daniel Cox 33, 37,
JTB Photo Communications Inc. 2–3, 42;
Photos.com: 4, 34; **Shutterstock**: Karel
Broz 5, 45, Florida Stock 18, Robynrg 9, 10,
Carolina K. Smith, M. D. 30, Martin Trajkovski
13; **Still Pictures**: Malcolm Schuyl 29.

Contents

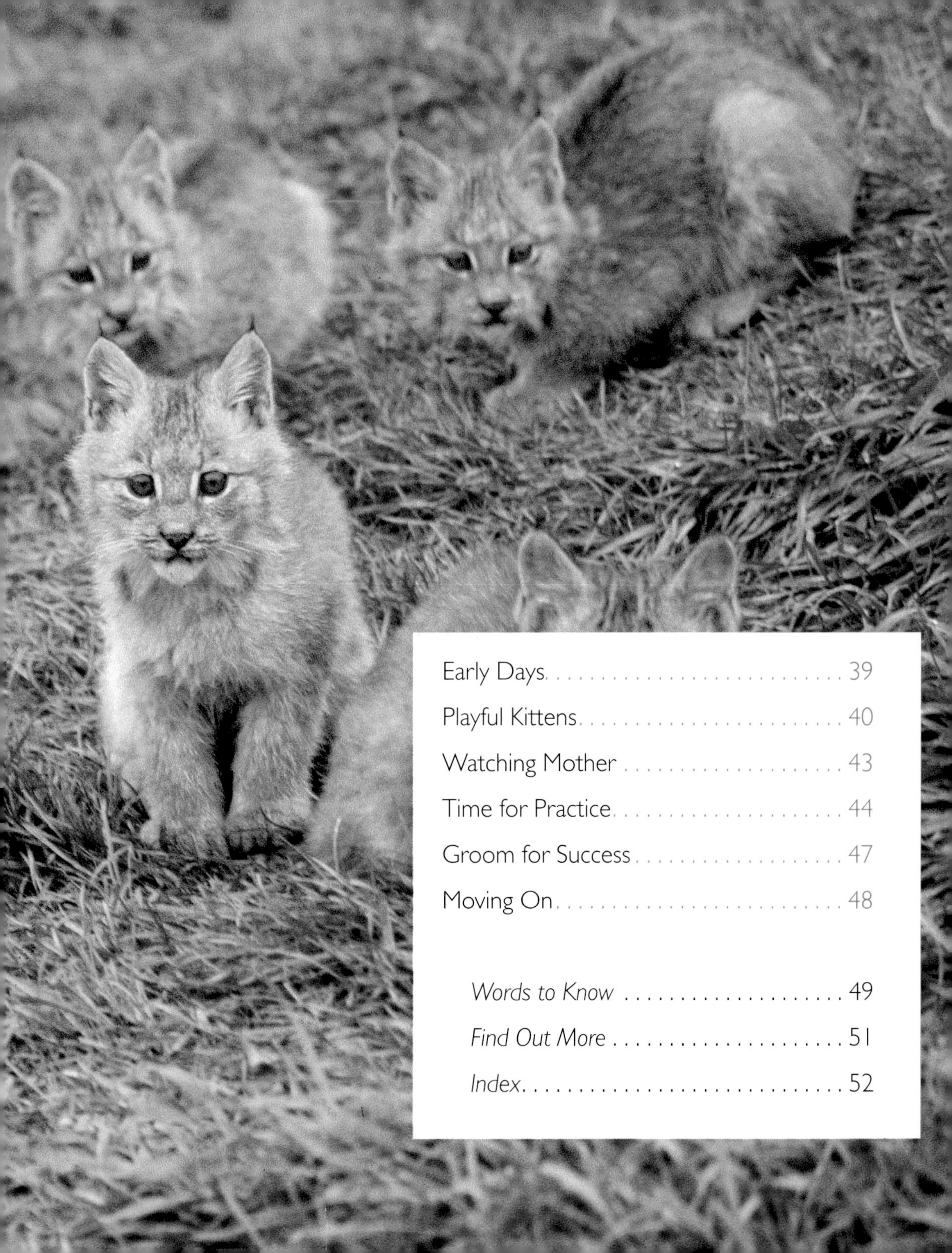

FACT FILE: Lynx

Class	Mammals (Mammalia)
Order	Carnivores (Carnivora)
Family	Cats (Felidae)
Genus	Lynx and bobcat (*Lynx*)
Species	Canadian lynx (*Lynx canadensis*), Eurasian lynx (*L. lynx*), Iberian lynx (*L. pardinus*), and bobcat (*L. rufus*)
World distribution	Canadian lynx live in northern North America; Eurasian lynx live in Eastern Europe and northern Asia; Iberian lynx are found in Spain and Portugal; bobcats range from Canada to Mexico
Habitat	Forests and scrublands
Distinctive physical characteristics	Smallish body with long legs and big paws; short tail; black tufts on ears; furry sideburns
Habits	Lynx live alone; they have a territory; they hunt mostly at night
Diet	Birds, rodents, rabbits, and small deer

Introduction

Lynx are easy to recognize with their black ear tufts, furry sideburns, long legs, and huge paws. But these shy and secretive cats are very difficult to see in the wild. When a human enters its **territory**, a lynx stays hidden. Its fur color blends in with the surroundings. Intruders are usually unaware of the lynx, but the lynx will be watching silently from a tree or under a bush. The lynx stays in hiding until nightfall. Then, it will wander stealthily through its territory, searching for **prey**.

Using its sharp eyes and ears, a lynx will detect a human long before it is seen itself.

A Canadian lynx
climbs through
a tree. Lynx
usually live in
forested areas.

Cat Family

There are 37 members of the cat family. They include lions, tigers, cheetahs, jaguars, and the house cats people keep as pets. Cats are meat eaters, or **carnivores**. Their super senses, large teeth, strong jaws, and sharp claws make cats well suited to killing and eating other animals.

In North America, there are three **species** of wild cats. The biggest is the cougar, also called the puma or mountain lion. The other two cats are types of lynx: the Canadian lynx and the bobcat. Cougars are easy to tell apart from lynx. They are much bigger and have a long tail. All lynx have a short, or "bobbed" tail. Cougars are also one of the lynx's main enemies. There are two other species of lynx: the Eurasian lynx of Eastern Europe and Asia and the Iberian lynx from Spain and Portugal.

Canadian Lynx

The Canadian lynx lives in the northern region of North America, ranging from Alaska across most of Canada and into the northern states of the United States. It is most at home in forested areas, but the lynx also survives along the edge of the **tundra** and in marshes and wetlands.

A Canadian lynx grows to a little more than 3 feet (90 cm) long and weighs up to 38 pounds (17 kg). As with all lynx, the Canadian species has the distinctive black tufts on the top of its triangular ears. It also has ruffs of hair that look like sideburns on either side of its head. The Canadian lynx has yellowish brown fur, but this might be darker on the cat's upper body. Many of the cats have faint spots on their coat. Canadian lynx are shy animals. They stay away from houses and any place humans might be, so people rarely see them in the wild.

The Canadian lynx's coat is less spotty than that of the other species of lynx.

There are about one
million bobcats living
in the United States,
but they keep well
out of sight.

Bobcats

Bobcats range from southern Canada to southern Mexico. In the United States they are most common in southeastern states and even venture into towns at night to hunt. They are slightly smaller than Canadian lynx. The bobcat's ear tufts are shorter than those of other lynx. Its tail is also longer, and it has dark rings around it. There are also distinctive black bands of fur on its legs. The fur is sometimes reddish. For this reason, the bobcat is also known as the red lynx.

Like all types of lynx, bobcats are strict meat eaters. They hunt rabbits and hares, but will also make do with smaller prey, such as squirrels and mice. When their main foods are difficult to find, bobcats turn their attention to larger animals, such as small deer.

Largest Lynx

The Eurasian lynx is the biggest lynx species. The males grow to 48 inches (1.3 m) long and can weigh up to 66 pounds (30 kg). Because of their larger size, Eurasian lynx are able to catch bigger prey. As well as hares, the Eurasian cats regularly kill deer. As with all species of lynx, the adult females are about one-third smaller than the males.

Eurasian lynx live in pine forests and thick scrub in eastern Europe and northern Asia. They were once common throughout Europe but were wiped out in western and central European countries due to hunting and **habitat** loss. However, lynx have since been reintroduced to some countries such as Switzerland and Germany. So far, the cats have been breeding successfully in remote mountain areas.

The Eurasian lynx
is a protected
species in Europe,
but is still hunted
in parts of Asia.

13

The Iberian lynx is now being bred in captivity. Biologists hope this will save the species from extinction.

Spanish Cat

With its distinctive leopardlike spots, the Iberian lynx is the most striking type of lynx. It is also the smallest species. The cats live in just a few locations in Spain and Portugal, which together are known as Iberia.

The Iberian lynx is the rarest cat species in the world. There are thought to be between 100 and 1,000 left in the wild. If this lynx does become extinct, it will be the first cat species to disappear since the saber-tooth tiger, which died out about 8,000 years ago.

There are many reasons for the Iberian lynx's decline, including hunting, habitat loss, poisoning, and road accidents. The biggest reason, however, has been a big drop in the number of wild rabbits—the cat's main source of food. The rabbits have been killed by diseases.

Legs and Paws

Lynx have long legs and very big paws, which allow them to move easily and swiftly in deep snow. The long legs let the animal cover larger distances in a few strides. Lynx run in a clumsy gallop, but they can cover ground quickly. They can jump high, too, bounding over boulders and fallen tree trunks when chasing a rabbit or escaping a **predator**.

The big paws act like snowshoes. Their large area spreads out the lynx's weight when walking over deep snow. That means that the cat does not sink too deep into the snow. The thick fur on the paws is also very helpful for keeping the feet warm. That is a must because temperatures drop as low as -30°F (-35°C) in winter.

Being able to
move across
snow ensures
that lynx can
hunt throughout
the winter.

A lynx's silver winter coat is formed by a mixture of white and gray hairs with black tips.

Furry Felines

A lynx's fur coat has two layers. The longer outer layer is made up of **guard hairs**. These hairs, which grow as long as 4 inches (10 cm), protect the cat from cold, icy winds. They also shed water easily, so that rain does not reach the lynx's skin. Beneath the guard hairs is a fluffy, dense layer of shorter hairs called underfur. These hairs trap air inside them and act like a blanket around the cat. A lynx's winter coat is usually silver-gray, a similar color to the surrounding ice and rocks.

In summer the lynx sheds, or **molts**, some of its longer hairs, and a shorter coat grows. This summer fur is often a different color from the winter coat. It might be light brown with faint spots. This coloration allows the lynx to blend into its forest surroundings now that the snow has melted. The **camouflaged** cat is then almost invisible to its prey.

Hunting Machines

All species of cats are skillful hunters. Their sharp senses and sharper claws and teeth, make these nimble creatures top predators wherever they live. A lynx's big furry paws muffle its footsteps, which allow it to sneak up on rabbits or mice unheard. Before the lynx pounces, it crouches low, intently watching its prey and waiting for the right moment to attack. The lynx's forward-facing eyes can judge distances very accurately as the cat closes in. The prey usually does not stand a chance when the lynx pounces. Within seconds, it is struggling in the lynx's strong jaws. The lynx kills most prey by breaking its neck with a swift bite. The cat will kill larger prey, such as deer, by crushing its neck with its powerful jaws. That squeezes the prey's windpipe so it cannot breathe, and it eventually suffocates.

A lynx will scan an area with its moveable ears to pick up the rustles made by prey.

Snowshoe hares are active all year round, so Canadian lynx prey on them even in the middle of winter.

Ten-year Cycle

In winter, Canadian lynx feed mostly on snowshoe hares. Scientists have known about the relationship between the number of snowshoe hares and the number of Canadian lynx for a long time.

When there is plenty of food for the hares, they breed very rapidly. Lynx then have plenty of prey, and female lynx produce more young. But as the number of hares rises, there is less food for the hares to go around. Soon the number of hares starts to fall. There is then less food for all the lynx. The numbers of lynx then also decreases as younger lynx find it hard to survive and female lynx have fewer **kittens**.

The numbers of hares and lynx drop rapidly, or crash. With few lynx around, the hare population can grow again. Soon the number of lynx is rising once again, too.

From studying old records of the numbers of hares and lynx caught by fur trappers, scientists believe that the cycle lasts about 10 years.

In the Trees

Like domestic cats, lynx are skilled tree climbers. Lynx often use a tree as a lookout for prey. The lynx depends almost entirely on its sense of sight when hunting. Most other forest predators, such as wolves or bears, rely on their amazing sense of smell to find prey.

A lynx will also head for a tree if it is being chased by a wolf or brown bear. The cat will then wait for the wolf or brown bear, which cannot climb trees, to give up and go away. Cougars will kill lynx given the chance. These larger hunters can climb trees, too, so lynx need to find another escape route. Even though they do not like water, a desperate lynx or bobcat will splash through a stream or river to escape its more powerful relatives.

Night Sight

Lynx hunt mainly during the night, although many prefer to search for food at dusk and dawn. Because they hunt by sight, lynx have very sensitive eyes. At night in the forests and scrublands where lynx live, there are no streetlights, just starlight and moonlight. So the lynx's **pupils** grow very wide to let as much light as possible into the eyes. That is enough to give the cat night vision that is as good as human vision is during the day. However, cats do not have color vision. Instead, they see the world in black and white and shades of gray.

A lynx holds a pheasant in its jaws. The cat can spring into the air and snatch flying birds.

Wonderful Whiskers

Lynx also use touch to help them hunt in darkness. On either side of the cat's nose are long sensitive hairs called whiskers. The lynx uses these in places that are too dark to see anything, such as in thick scrub or a cave.

The whiskers stick out as far as the cat's shoulders—the widest part of its body. If the whiskers on both sides of the face brush against rocks or stems, the cat knows it is time to stop. The space ahead is too small for the lynx's body to squeeze through. The cat will then have to find an alternate way or turn back. Lynx have excellent hearing, too.

A lynx's whiskers are ordinary hairs, but they have several sensors at their base, which pick up any movements the hairs make.

A male lynx patrols
his territory regularly.
He travels as much
as 12 miles (19 km)
at a time.

No Trespassing!

Male lynx have a home area, or territory, which they defend against other males. The size of the territory depends on the amount of food available in it. If there is plenty of prey, the cat's territory is small. If prey is scarce, such as in cold northern areas, the territory is much larger. A lynx marks out the boundary of its territory with special signs. It makes scratch marks on tree trunks and then sprays the marks with its urine. That sign is called a scent post, or **scrape**. It warns other male lynx to keep out.

The scrapes are resprayed regularly as the lynx patrols his territory. If the scent fades on a scrape, there is a danger that another male will move into the territory.

Female lynx are allowed to move in and out of a male's territory. They have smaller territories that overlap with a male's. He doesn't mind. When the **mating season** comes, he will not have to look far for a **mate**.

Finding a Mate

All species of lynx have their mating season between January and March. The male lynx lets out high-pitched howls to attract neighboring females. The howling also serves to warn off other males. However, there are still often fierce catfights between rival males. They hiss, spit, screech, and lash at each other with their sharp claws. Scratches and other injuries are common. Eventually the weaker male backs off and disappears into the forest to lick his wounds. The winning male then continues to track down the nearest female, who answers to his calls with her own howls.

When two lynx meet they pause to smell each other and compare their odors to scent posts in the area.

After staying with its mate
for a few days or weeks, a
male lynx will look for other
females to breed with.

Short Courtship

Lynx are solitary animals. They spend most of their life alone, prowling through their territory. The exceptions to that are when adults pair up in the mating season, and when female lynx raise their young.

A breeding pair of lynx will share each other's company from anywhere between two days and a few weeks. The males eventually leave their mates to look for any other females in the area. If the male stays with the female for too long, she will try to get rid of him by hissing, scratching, and biting. She doesn't want him around when her young are born. Male lynx play no part in bringing up their young. And like many other species of cats, a male might kill the kittens, even if they are his own.

Newborn Lynx

Female lynx are pregnant for about two months. When the female is ready to give birth, she finds a **den**. The den has to be somewhere dry that is also well hidden from predators. It also has to be near a plentiful supply of prey. Lynx usually make their dens under a big log or in a cave.

Lynx have litters of between one and five young. The newborn cats, or kittens, are tiny compared to their mother. They weigh about 12 ounces (330 g). The newborns are covered in fluffy gray fur and are almost entirely helpless. They can neither see nor hear. But the kittens can smell and they follow the scent of milk to find their mother's teats. Soon they are **nursing**, or drinking, her rich milk.

Many lynx kittens are born in early spring when it is still quite chilly. Fortunately, they already have a lot of fur to keep them warm.

Lynx kittens have large paws, just like an adult lynx.

Early Days

By two weeks, the lynx kittens can see and hear. However, they are still too little to leave the warmth and comfort of the den. The kittens stay home for at least the first month. They will stay longer if the spring weather is late. They spend their days sleeping and nursing. The fat and proteins in the milk help them grow fast.

The hungry mother starts to make trips outside the den to hunt for herself. However, she does not go far from the den. She is fiercely protective of her precious young. Should another lynx, wolf, cougar, or other enemies come too close to the den, she will fight them to protect her young.

Playful Kittens

After about four to six weeks in the den, the kittens make their first ventures outside. Their time outside is great fun. They run and jump, chasing one another and any insects that fly by. They practice the things that adults do, too, such as climbing tree stumps and play-fighting.

All the play eventually tires them out. They then return to their den for a snooze, nestled in their mother's fur.

The kittens nurse for about five months. But when they are three or four months old, the mother begins to bring her litter meat and bones to eat. Gnawing on tough bones is good for the kittens because it strengthens their jaws. They will need strong jaws to kill prey of their own one day.

At first the kittens
spend just a few hours
each day outside. But by
midsummer they spend
most of their time away
from the den.

It takes three months of hunting lessons before kittens are good enough to find enough food for themselves.

Watching Mother

By two months old, the kittens have lost their fluffy baby fur. They now have a beautiful spotted coat that looks similar to the summer fur of their parents. As the kittens get older, the spots will gradually grow fainter.

The kittens are now ready to learn how to hunt. They begin to accompany their mother on short hunting trips around the den. They have to pay close attention. These lessons are vital for their survival. Often she hides the kittens nearby so they can watch as she **stalks** or lies in ambush before pouncing on an unsuspecting hare or rabbit.

Time for Practice

When the kittens first start hunting, they begin by stalking small animals, such as mice and voles. Hunting takes a certain amount of practice to perfect, and the prey often escape the clutches of the kittens. But the cats learn from their mistakes. Soon they are almost as accomplished at hunting as their mother.

Sometimes the mother and her kittens work together to catch prey, just like a pride of lions. The family spreads out to form a line as it moves slowly through the undergrowth. The formation increases the chance of finding and then catching fast-running prey. If one of the cats startles a hare or rabbit, it will most likely run out into the open. The chances are the terrified prey will run straight into the path of one of the other lynx in the line.

As a lynx gets older,
the tufts on its ears
get longer.

A lynx grows two fresh coats each year, and a young kitten needs to know how to keep it clean.

Groom for Success

While still living with their mother, the kittens learn to clean, or groom, themselves. When they were very young, their mother licked the babies clean. Now the kittens spend a lot of time grooming themselves. Like all cats, lynx have a rough tongue. It is used to lick scraps of meat off of bones, but the tongue is also ideal for combing hair. The kittens lick the back of one of their front paws and use it to sponge their face.

Dirty fur might get infested with bugs or bacteria. That could make the hair fall out— and that is not a good thing when the cold winter weather is a few months away. Badly kept fur is usually a sign that an animal is ill and can no longer look after itself. Mates and rivals will not be impressed by dirty hair.

Moving On

Young lynx stay with their mothers for their first winter. In early spring, the young cats will leave to make their own way in the world. By that time, the mother is ready to mate again and doesn't want her growing kittens around. In addition, her next mate might attack them.

If young lynx have learned their hunting skills well, they will not go hungry. However, if their favorite prey is in short supply, they might find it too tough to set up on their own.

Young female lynx usually set up a territory near their mothers. Males have to travel farther to find a home. By next spring, the young lynx will be ready to start families of their own. If a lynx survives its first year in the wild, it will probably live for 10 to 12 years.

Words to Know

Camouflaged   Colored or marked to allow an
animal to blend into its surroundings.

Carnivores   Meat-eating animals.

Den   An animal's home.

Guard hairs   Long, coarse hair that make up the
outer layer of a lynx's coat.

Habitat   A place where an animal lives.

Kittens   Young lynx.

Mate   Either of a breeding pair; to come
together to produce young.

Mating season   The time of the year when animals
come together to produce young.

Molts   Sheds fur and replaces it with
another coat.

49

Nursing	Drinking milk from the mother's body.
Predator	An animal that hunts other animals.
Prey	An animal that is hunted and eaten by another animal.
Pupils	The opening at the front of each eye through which light enters.
Scrape	A sign that marks the boundaries of an animal's territory.
Species	The scientific word for animals of the same type that can breed together.
Stalks	Sneaks up on or follows prey silently.
Territory	An area that an animal or group of animals lives in and often defends from other animals of the same kind.
Tundra	Cold, flat, treeless region in the far north.

Find Out More

Books

Gentle, V. *Lynxes*. Milwaukee, Wisconsin: Gareth
Stevens, 2002.

St. Pierre, S. *Lynx*. Chicago, Illinois: Heinemann
Library, 2001.

Web sites

Bobcat Printout
enchantedlearning.com/subjects/mammals/cats/bobcat/
Bobcatprintout.shtml
Facts about bobcats and a picture to print.

Lynx Profile
animals.nationalgeographic.com/animals/mammals/
lynx.html
Tons of facts about lynx, including a recording of
a lynx growling.

Index

52